CW00956242

A Little

of

Consolation

by David Coombs

*All booklets are published thanks to the
generous support of the members of the
Catholic Truth Society*

CATHOLIC TRUTH SOCIETY
PUBLISHERS TO THE HOLY SEE

Contents

∞

Introductory Note

Through its liturgy and public prayers the Catholic Church powerfully and constantly supports the dead and the dying.

But, the needs of the bereaved, they who mourn, are strangely neglected: an unexpected human and spiritual void that has led me to compile this little publication. Its message is one of personal consolation and thus of hope. To these purposes, a hint or sense of divine mystery is present in all the chosen prayers and readings.

This offering, which has been many years in the making, contains much that will be familiar and some that may not be, none previously brought together in this form, as far as I know.

Intended for personal yet purposeful browsing from time to time, over the needful span, it might be helpful in the first instance to begin with a prayer or a psalm, and then to move on to one or other of the scriptural readings as want, mood or inclination suggests.

AMDG, November 2010

∞

∞Blessed are those who mourn∞

*I*n the name of the Father,
and of the Son
and of the Holy Spirit.
Amen.

∞

*E*ternal rest grant unto them, O Lord.
And let perpetual light shine upon them.
May they rest in peace.
Amen.

∞

Seeing the crowds, Jesus went onto the mountain.
And when he was seated his disciples came to him.
Then he began to speak. This is what he taught them:
Blessed are those who mourn: they shall be
comforted.

Matthew 5: 1 – 5

∞

I am the resurrection and the Life. Anyone who
believes in me, even though that person dies, will
live, and whoever lives and believes in me
will never die.

John 11: 25

∞

❧Prayers❧

*L*ord, listen to my prayer: turn your ear
to my appeal. You are faithful,
you are just; give answer.
I remember the days that are past:
I ponder all your works.
I muse on what your hand has wrought
and to you I stretch out my hands.
Like a parched land my soul thirsts for you.
Lord, make haste and give me answer:
for my spirit fails within me.

Psalm 142, vv. 1,3,6,7

❧

Our Father

*O*ur Father, who art in heaven,
hallowed be thy name.
Thy kingdom come, Thy will be done
on earth as it is in heaven.
Give us this day our daily bread,
and forgive us our trespasses,
as we forgive those who trespass against us.
And lead us not into temptation,
but deliver us from evil.
Amen

❧

∞

Hail Mary

*Hail Mary, full of grace,
the Lord is with thee:
blessed art thou among women,
and blessed is the fruit of thy womb, Jesus.
Holy Mary, Mother of God,
pray for us sinners now,
and at the hour of our death.
Amen*

∞

Memorarae

*Remember, O most loving Virgin Mary,
that it is a thing unheard of
that anyone ever had recourse to your protection,
implored your help, or sought your intercession,
and was left forsaken.
Filled therefore with confidence in your goodness
I fly to you, O Mother, Virgin of Virgins.
To you I come, before you I stand,
a sorrowful sinner.
Despise not my poor words,
O Mother of the Word of God,
but graciously hear and grant my prayer.
Amen*

∞

∞

*Receive, Lord,
in tranquillity and peace,
the souls of your servants
who have departed out of this present life
to be with you.
Give them the life that knows no age,
the good things that do not pass away;
through Jesus Christ our Lord.*

Saint Ignatius Loyola

∞

*Let nothing disturb thee,
let nothing affright thee,
all passeth away;
God alone abideth.
Patience obtaineth all things.
He who hath God
can want for nothing.
God alone sufficeth.*

Saint Teresa of Avila

∞

∞

Creed

I believe in God, the Father almighty,
creator of heaven and earth. I believe in
Jesus Christ, his only son, our Lord.
He was conceived by the power of the Holy Spirit
and born of the Virgin Mary.
He suffered under Pontius Pilate, was crucified,
died and was buried. He descended to the dead.
On the third day he rose again. He ascended into
heaven, and is seated at the right hand of the
Father. He will come again to judge the living
and the dead. I believe in the
Holy Spirit, the holy Catholic Church, the
communion of saints, the forgiveness of sins,
the resurrection of the body, and life everlasting.
Amen.

∞

∾From the Psalms∾

Psalm 129

O ut of the depths I cry to you,
  O Lord, Lord hear my voice!
O let your ears be attentive to the voice
of my pleading.

If you, O Lord, should mark our guilt,
Lord who would survive?
But with you is found forgiveness:
for this we revere you.

My soul is waiting for the Lord,
I count on his word.
My soul is longing for the Lord more than
watchman for daybreak.
(Let the watchman count on daybreak
and Israel on the Lord.)

Because with the Lord there is mercy
and fullness of redemption,
Israel indeed he will redeem
from all its iniquity.

∾

Psalm 141

With all my voice I cry to the Lord,
with all my voice I entreat the Lord.
I pour out my trouble before him:
I tell him all my distress while my spirit faints
within me. But you, O Lord, know my path.

On the way where I shall walk
they have hidden a snare to entrap me.
Look on my right and see:
there is no one who takes my part.
I have no means of escape,
not one who cares for my soul.

I cry to you, O Lord. I have said:
"You are my refuge, all I have in the land
of living."Listen then to my cry
for I am in the depths of distress.

Rescue me from those who pursue me
for they are stronger than I.
Bring my soul out of this prison
and then I shall praise your name.
Around me the just will assemble
because of your goodness to me.

∽From the Prophet Isaiah∾

Unhappy creature, storm-tossed, unpitied,
look, I shall lay your stones on agates
and your foundations on sapphires.
I shall make your battlements rubies,
your gateways firestone
and your entire wall precious stones.
All your children will be taught by the Lord
and great will be your children's prosperity.
In saving justice you will be made firm,
free from oppression: you will have nothing to fear;
free from terror: it will not approach you.
Should anyone attack you, that will not be my doing,
and whoever does attack you, for your sake will fall.
I created the smith
who blows on the charcoal-fire
to produce a weapon for his use;
I also created the destroyer to ruin it.
No weapon forged against you will succeed.
Any voice raised against you in court you will refute.
Such is the lot of the servants of the Lord,
the saving justice I assure them,
declares the Lord.

Isaiah 54: 11 -17

∽

Seek out the Lord while he is still to be found,
call to him while he is still near.
Let the wicked abandon his way
and the evil one his thoughts.
Let him turn back to the Lord
who will take pity on him,
to our God, for he is rich in forgiveness;
for my thoughts are not your thoughts
and your ways are not my ways,
declares the Lord.
For the heavens are as high above earth
as my ways are above your ways,
my thoughts above your thoughts.
For, as the rain and the snow come down
from the sky and do not return
before having watered the earth,
fertilising it and making it germinate
to provide seed for the sower and seed to eat,
so it is with the word that goes from my mouth:
it will not return to me unfulfilled
or before having carried out my good pleasure
and having achieved what it was sent to do.
Yes, you will go out with joy
and be led away in safety.

Mountains and hills will break into joyful cries
before you and all the trees of the countryside
clap their hands.
Cypress will grow instead of thorns,
myrtle instead of nettles.
And this will be fame for the Lord,
an eternal monument never to be effaced.

Isaiah 55: 6 - 13

∽The Patriarch Abraham∾

The Lord appeared to Abraham at the Oak of Mamre while he was sitting by the entrance of the tent during the hottest part of the day. He looked up, and there he saw three men standing near him. As soon as he saw them he ran from the entrance of the tent to greet them, and bowed to the ground. 'My lord,' he said, 'if I find favour with you, please do not pass your servant by. Let me have a little water brought, and you can wash your feet and have a rest under the tree. Let me fetch a little bread and you can refresh yourselves before going any further, now that you have come in your servant's direction.' They replied, 'Do as you say.'

Abraham hurried to the tent and said to his wife Sarah, 'Quick, knead three measures of best flour and make loaves.' Then running to the herd, Abraham took a fine and tender calf and gave it to the servant, who hurried to prepare it. Then taking curds, milk and the calf which had been prepared, he laid all before them, and they ate while he remained standing near them under the tree.

From there the men set out and arrived within sight of Sodom, with Abraham accompanying them to speed them on their way. Now the Lord had wondered,' Shall I conceal from Abraham what I am going to do, as Abraham will become a great and powerful nation and that all nations on earth will bless themselves by him? For I have singled him out to command his sons and his family after him to keep the way of the Lord by doing what is upright and just, so that the Lord can carry out for Abraham what he has promised him.' Then the Lord said, 'The outcry against Sodom and Gomorrah is so great and their sin is so grave, that I shall go down and see whether or not their actions are at all as the outcry reaching me would suggest. Then I shall know.'

While the men left there and went to Sodom, the Lord remained in Abraham's presence. Abraham stepped forward and said. 'Will you really destroy the upright with the guilty? Suppose there are fifty upright people in the city. Will you really destroy it? Will you not spare the place for the sake of the fifty upright in it? Do not think of doing such a thing: to put the upright to death with the guilty, so that upright and guilty fare alike! Is the judge of the whole world not to act justly?' The Lord replied, 'If I find fifty upright people in the city of Sodom, I will spare the whole place because of them.'

Abraham spoke up and said, 'It is presumptuous of me to speak to the Lord, I who am dust and ashes: Suppose the fifty upright were five short? Would you destroy the whole city because of five?' 'No,' he replied, 'I will not destroy it if I find forty-five there.'

Abraham persisted and said, 'Suppose there are forty to be found there?' 'I will not do it for the sake of the forty.'

Abraham said, 'I hope the Lord will not be angry if I go on: Suppose there are only thirty to be found there?' 'I will not do it,' he replied, 'if I find thirty there.' He said. 'It is presumptuous of me to speak to the Lord: Suppose there are only twenty there?' 'I will not destroy it,' he replied, 'for the sake of the twenty.' He said, 'I trust my Lord will not be angry if I speak once more: perhaps there will only be ten?' 'I will not destroy it,' he replied, 'for the sake of the ten.' When he had finished talking to Abraham the Lord went away, and Abraham returned home.

Next morning, Abraham hurried to the place where he had stood before the Lord and looking towards Sodom and Gomorrah and the whole area of the plain, he saw smoke rising from the ground like smoke from a furnace.

Thus it was, when God destroyed the cities of the plain, he did not forget Abraham and he rescued Lot from the midst of the overthrow, when he overthrew the cities where Lot was living.

Genesis 18: 1 - 8, 16 - 33. 19: 27 - 29

⣿From the Prophet Elijah⣿

Elijah was afraid and fled for his life into the desert, a day's journey, and sitting under a furze bush wished he was dead. 'Lord,' he said, 'I have had enough. Take my life; I am no better than my ancestors.' Then he lay down and went to sleep. Then all of a sudden an angel touched him and said, 'Get up and eat.' He looked round, and there at his head was a scone baked on hot stones, and a jar of water. He eat and drank and lay down again. But the Angel of the Lord came back a second time and touched him and said, 'Get up and eat, or the journey will be too long for you.' So he got up and ate and drank, and strengthened by that food he walked for forty days and forty nights until he reached Horeb, God's mountain.

There he went into a cave and spent the night there. Then the word of the Lord came to him saying, 'What are you doing here Elijah?' He replied, 'I am full of jealous zeal for the Lord God of Hosts, because the Israelites have abandoned your covenant, have torn down your altars and put your prophets to the sword. I am the only one left, and now they want to kill me.' Then he was told, 'Go out and stand on the mountain before the Lord.' For at that moment the Lord was going by. A mighty hurricane split the mountains and shattered the rocks before the Lord. But the Lord was not in the hurricane. And after the hurricane, an earthquake. But the Lord was not in the earthquake. And after the earthquake, fire. But the Lord was not in the fire. And after the fire, a light murmuring sound. And when Elijah heard this, he covered his face with his cloak and went out and stood at the entrance of the cave. Then a voice came to him, which said, 'What are you doing here, Elijah?'

I *Kings* 19: 3, 4 - 13

In the sixth month the angel Gabriel was sent by God to a town in Galilee called Nazareth, to a virgin betrothed to a man named Joseph, of the house of David: and the virgin's name was Mary. He went in and said to her, 'Rejoice, you who enjoy God's favour! The Lord is with you.' She was deeply disturbed by these words and asked herself what this greeting could mean, but the angel said to her, 'Mary, do not be afraid; you have won God's favour. Look! You are to conceive in your womb and bear a son and you must name him Jesus. He will be great and will be called Son of the Most High. The Lord God will give him the throne of his ancestor David; he will rule over the House of Jacob for ever and his reign will have no end.'

Mary said to the angel, 'But how can this come about, since I have no knowledge of man?' The angel answered, 'The Holy Spirit will come upon you, and the power of the Most High will cover you with its shadow. And so the child will be holy and will be called Son of God. And I tell you this too: your cousin Elizabeth also, in her old age, has conceived a son, and she whom her people called barren is now in her sixth month, for nothing is impossible to God.' Mary said, 'You see before you the Lord's servant, let it happen to me as you have said.' And the angel left her.

Luke 1: 26 - 38

∽The Visitation∾

Mary set out at that time and went as quickly as she could into the hill country to a town in Judah. She went into Zechariah's house and greeted Elizabeth. Now it happened that as soon as Elizabeth heard Mary's greeting, the child leapt in her womb and Elizabeth was filled with the Holy Spirit. She gave a loud cry and said, 'Of all women you are the most blessed, and blessed is the fruit of your womb. Why should I be honoured with a visit from the mother of my Lord? Look, the moment your greeting reached my ears, the child in my womb leapt for joy. Yes, blessed is she who believed that the promise made her by the Lord would be fulfilled.' And Mary said:

My soul proclaims the greatness of the Lord
and my spirit rejoices in God my Saviour;
because he has looked upon the humiliation
of his servant.
Yes, from now onwards all generations
will call me blessed,
for the Almighty has done great things for me.
Holy is his name, and his faithful love
extends age after age
to those who fear him
he has used the power of his arm.
He has routed the arrogant of heart

He has pulled down princes from their thrones
and raised high the lowly.
He has filled the starving with good things,
sent the rich away empty.
He has come to the help of Israel his servant,
mindful of his faithful love
– according to the promise he made
to our ancestors – of his mercy to Abraham
and to his descendants for ever.

Mary stayed with her some three months and then
went home.

Luke 1: 39 - 56

❦The Nativity❦

Now it happened that at this time Caesar Augustus issued a decree that a census should be made of the whole inhabited world. This census - the first - while Quirinius was governor of Syria, and everyone went to be registered, each to his own town. So Joseph set out from the town of Nazareth in Galilee for Judaea, to David's town called Bethlelem, since he was of David's House and line, in order to be registered together with Mary, his betrothed, who was with child. Now it happened that, while they were there, the time came for her to have her child, and she gave birth to her son, her first-born. She wrapped him in swaddling clothes and laid him in a manger because there was no room for them in the living-space. In the countryside close by there were shepherds out in the fields keeping guard over their sheep during the watches of the night. An angel of the Lord stood over them and the glory of the Lord shone round them. They were terrified, but the angel said, 'Do not be afraid. Look, I bring you news of great joy, a joy to be shared by the whole people. Today in the town of David a Saviour has been born to you; he is Christ the Lord. And here is a sign for you: you will find a baby wrapped in swaddling clothes and lying in a manger.' And all at once with the angel there was a great throng of the hosts of heaven, praising God with the words:

Glory to God in the highest heaven,
and on earth peace for those he favours.

Now it happened that when the angels had gone from them into heaven, the shepherds said to one another, 'Let us go to Bethlehem and see this event which the Lord has made known to us.' So they hurried away and found Mary and Joseph, and the baby lying in a manger. When they saw the child they repeated what they had been told about him, and everyone who heard it was astonished at what the shepherds said to them. As for Mary, she treasured all these things and pondered them in her heart. And the shepherds went back glorifying and praising God for all they heard and seen, just as they had been told.

Luke 2: 1 – 20

∾Jesus walks on the water∾

Jesus made the disciples get into the boat and go on
ahead to the other side while he sent the crowds
away. After sending the crowds away he went up into
the hills by himself to pray. When evening came, he
was there alone, while the boat, by now some
furlongs from land, was hard pressed by rough waves,
for there was a head-wind. In the fourth watch of the
night he came towards them, walking on the sea, and
when the disciples saw him walking on the sea they
were terrified. 'It is a ghost,' they said, and cried out in
fear. But at once Jesus called out to them, saying,
'Courage! It's me! Don't be afraid.' It was Peter who
answered. 'Lord,' he said, 'if it is you, tell me to come
to you across the water.' Jesus said, 'Come'. Then
Peter got out of the boat and started walking across
the water, but then noticing the wind, he took fright
and began to sink. 'Lord,' he cried, 'save me.' Jesus
put out his hand at once and held him. 'You have so
little faith,' he said, 'why did you doubt?' And as they
got into the boat the wind dropped. The men in the
boat bowed down before him and said, 'Truly, you
are the Son of God.'

Matthew 14: 22 - 33

∾

∽The labourers in the vineyard∽

Jesus said to his disciples: Now the kingdom of Heaven is like a landowner going out at daybreak to hire workers for his vineyard. He made an agreement with the workers for one denarius a day and sent them to his vineyard. Going out at about the third hour he saw others standing idle in the market place and said to them, 'You go to my vineyard too and I will give you a fair wage.' So they went. At about the sixth hour and again at about the ninth hour, he went out and did the same. Then at about the eleventh hour he went out and found more men standing around, and he said to them, 'Why have you been standing here idle all day?' 'Because no one has hired us,' they answered. He said to them, 'You go into my vineyard too.' In the evening, the owner of the vineyard said to his bailiff, 'Call the workers and pay them their wages, starting with the last arrivals and ending with the first.' So those that were hired at about the eleventh hour came forward and received one denarius each. When the first came, they expected to get more, but they too received one denarius each. They took it, but grumbled at the landowner saying, 'The men who came last have done only one hour, and you have treated them the same as us, though we have done a heavy day's work in all the heat.' He answered one of them and said, 'My friend, I am not being unjust to you; did we not agree on one denarius? Take your earnings and go. I choose to pay the last comer as much as I pay you. Have I no right to do what I like with my own? Why should you be envious because I am generous? Thus the last will be first, and the first, last.'

Matthew 20: 1 - 16

ᕫThe story of Lazarusᕫ

There was a man named Lazarus of Bethany, the village of Mary and her sister, Martha, and he was ill. It was the same Mary, the sister of the sick man Lazarus, who anointed the Lord with ointment and wiped his feet with her hair. The sisters sent this message to Jesus, 'Lord the man you love is ill.' On receiving the message, Jesus said, 'This sickness will not end in death, but it is for God's glory so that through it the Son of God may be glorified.'

Jesus loved Martha and her sister and Lazarus, yet when he heard he was ill he stayed where he was for two more days before saying to the disciples, 'Let us go back to Judea.' The disciples said, 'Rabbi, it is not long since the Jews were trying to stone you; are you going back there again?' Jesus replied:

Are there not twelve hours in the day?
No one who walks in the daytime stumbles,
having the light of this world to see by;
anyone who walks around at night stumbles,
having no light as a guide.

He said that and then added, 'Our friend Lazarus is at rest; I am going to wake him.' The disciples said to him, 'Lord if he is at rest he will be saved.' Jesus was speaking of the death of Lazarus, but they thought that by 'rest' he meant 'sleep'; so Jesus put it plainly, 'Lazarus is dead; and for your sake I am glad I was not there because now you will believe. But let us go to him.' Then Thomas - known as the Twin - said to the other disciples, 'Let us also go to die with him.'

On arriving, Jesus found that Lazarus had been in the tomb for four days already. Bethany is only about two miles from Jerusalem and many Jews had come to Martha and Mary to comfort them about their brother. When Martha heard that Jesus was coming she went to meet him. Mary remained sitting in the house. Martha said to Jesus, 'Lord if you had been here, my brother would not have died, but even now I know that God will grant whatever you ask of him.' Jesus said to her, 'Your brother will rise again.' Martha said, 'I know he will rise again at the resurrection on the last day.' Jesus said:

> I am the resurrection.
> Anyone who believes in me,
> even though that person dies, will live,
> and whoever lives and believes in me
> will never die.
> Do you believe this?

'Yes Lord,' she said, 'I believe that you are the Christ, the Son of God, the one who was to come into this world.'

When she had said this, she went and called her sister Mary, saying in a low voice, 'The Master is here and wants to see you.' Hearing this, Mary got up quickly and went to him. Jesus had not yet come into the village; he was still at the place where Martha had met him. When the Jews who were in the house comforting Mary saw her get up so quickly and go out, they followed her, thinking that she was going to the tomb to weep there.

Mary went to Jesus, and as soon as she saw him she threw herself at his feet, saying, 'Lord if you had been here, my brother would not have died.' At the sight of her tears, and those of the Jews who had come with her, Jesus was greatly distressed, and with a profound sigh he said, 'Where have you put him?' They said, 'Lord come and see.' Jesus wept; and the Jews said, 'See how much he loved him!' But there some who remarked, 'He opened the eyes of the blind man. Could he not have prevented this man's death?'

Sighing again, Jesus reached the tomb: it was a cave with a stone to close the opening. Jesus said, 'Take the stone away.' Martha, the dead man's sister, said to him, 'Lord by now he will smell; this is the fourth day since he died.' Jesus replied, 'Have I not told you that if you believe you will see the glory of God?' So they took the stone away. Then Jesus lifted up his eyes and said: Father, I thank you for hearing my prayer. I myself knew that you hear me always, but I speak for

the sake of all those who are standing around me, so
that they may believe it was you who sent me.

When he had said this, he cried in a loud voice,
'Lazarus, come out!' The dead man came out, his feet
and hands bound with strips of material, and a cloth
over his face. Jesus said, 'Unbind him, let him
go free.'

John 11:1 - 44

⟐Jesus and Nicodemus⟐

There was one of the Pharisees called Nicodemus, a leader of the Jews, who came to Jesus by night and said, 'Rabbi, we know that you have come from God as a teacher; for no one could perform the signs that you do unless God were with him.' Jesus answered: 'In all truth I tell you, no one can see the kingdom of God without being born from above.' Nicodemus said, 'How can anyone who is already old be born? Is it possible to go back into the womb again and be born?' Jesus replied: 'In all truth I tell you, no one can enter the kingdom of God without being born through water and the Spirit; what is born of human nature is human; what is born of the Spirit is spirit. Do not be surprised when I say: You must be born from above. The wind blows where it pleases; you can hear its sound, but you cannot hear where it comes from or where it is going. So it is with everyone who is born of the Spirit.'

'How is that possible?' asked Nicodemus. Jesus replied, 'You are a Teacher of Israel, and you do not know these things! 'In all truth I tell you, we speak only about what we know and witness only to what we have seen and yet you people reject our evidence. If you do not believe me when I speak to you about earthly things, how will you believe me when I speak to you about heavenly things? No one has gone up to heaven except the one who came down from heaven, the Son of man; as Moses lifted up the snake in the desert, so must the Son of man be lifted up so that everyone who believes may have eternal life in him. For this is how God loved the world: he gave his only Son, so that everyone who believes in him may not perish but may have eternal life. For God sent his Son into the world not to judge the world, but so that through him the world might be saved. No one who believes in him will be judged; but whoever does not believe is judged already, because that person does not believe in the Name of God's only Son. And the judgement is this: though the light has come into the world people have preferred darkness to light because their deeds were evil.

And indeed, everybody who does wrong hates the light and avoids it, to prevent his actions from being shown up; but whoever does the truth comes out into the light, so that what he is doing may plainly appear as done in God.'

John 3: 1 - 21

⧼The garden of Gethsemane⧽

They came to a plot of land called Gethsemane, and Jesus said to his disciples, 'Stay here while I pray.' Then he took Peter and James and John with him. And he began to feel terror and anguish. And he said to them, 'My soul is sorrowful to the point of death. Wait here, and stay awake.' And going on a little further he threw himself on the ground and prayed that, if it were possible, this hour might pass him by. 'Abba, Father! he said, 'For you everything is possible. Take this cup away from me. But let it be as you, not I, would have it.'

Then an angel appeared to him, coming from heaven to give him strength. In his anguish he prayed even more earnestly, and his sweat fell to the ground like great drops of blood.

He came back and found them sleeping, and he said to Peter, 'Simon, are you asleep? Had you not the strength to stay awake one hour? Stay awake and pray not to be put to the test. The spirit is willing enough, but human nature is weak.' And he went away and prayed, saying the same words. And once more he came back and found them sleeping, their eyes were so heavy; and they could find no answer for him. He came back a third time and said to them, 'You can sleep on now and have your rest. It is all over. The hour has come. Now the Son of man is to be betrayed into the hands of sinners. Get up! let us go!'

From: *Mark* 14: 32 - 36. *Luke* 22: 43 - 44. *Mark* 14: 37 - 42

ᗗThe Crucifixionᗘ

The soldiers led Jesus away to the inner part of the palace, that is, the Praetorium, and called the whole cohort together. They dressed him up in purple, twisted some thorns into a crown and put it on him. And they began saluting him, 'Hail king of the Jews!' They struck his head with a reed and spat on him; and they went down on their knees to do him homage. And when they had finished making fun of him, they took off the purple and dressed him in his own clothes.

They led him out to crucify him. They enlisted a passer-by, Simon of Cyrene, father of Alexander and Rufus, who was coming in from the country, to carry his cross. They brought Jesus to the place called Golgotha, which means the place of the skull. They offered him wine mixed with myrrh, but he refused it. Then they crucified him. It was the third hour. And they crucified two bandits with him, one on his right and one on his left. Jesus said, 'Father forgive them; they do not know what they are doing.' Pilate wrote out a notice and had fixed to the cross; it ran 'Jesus the Nazarene, King of the Jews'. This notice was read by many of the Jews, because the place where Jesus was crucified was near the city, and the writing was in Hebrew, Latin and Greek. So the Jewish chief priests said to Pilate. 'You should not write "King of the Jews", but that the man said, "I am King of the Jews". 'Pilate answered, 'What I have written, I have written.'

When the soldiers had finished crucifying Jesus they took his clothing and divided it into four shares, one for each soldier. His undergarment was seamless, woven in one piece from neck to hem, so they said to one another, 'Instead of tearing it, let's throw dice to decide who is to have it.'

One of the criminals hanging there abused him: 'Are you not the Christ? Save yourself and us as well.' But the other spoke up and rebuked him. 'Have you no fear of God at all?' he said. 'You got the same sentence as he did, but in our case we deserved it: we are paying for what we did. But this man has done nothing wrong.' Then he said, 'Jesus, remember me when you come into your kingdom.' He answered him, 'In truth I tell you, today you will be with me in paradise.'

The passers-by jeered at him; they shook their heads and said, 'Aha! So you would destroy the Temple and rebuild it in three days! Then save yourself; come down from the cross!' The chief priests and the scribes mocked him among themselves in the same way with the words, 'He saved others, he cannot save himself. Let the Christ, the king of Israel, come down from the cross now, for us to see it and believe.'

Near the cross of Jesus stood his mother and his mother's sister, Mary the wife of Clopas, and Mary of Magdala. Seeing his mother and the disciple whom he loved standing near her, Jesus said to his mother, 'Woman, this is your son.' Then to the disciple he said, 'This is your mother.' And from that hour the disciple took her into his home.

After this, Jesus knew that everything had now been completely fulfilled, he said: 'I am thirsty.' A jar full of sour wine stood there; so, putting a sponge soaked in the wine on a hyssop stick, they held it up to his mouth. After Jesus had taken the wine he said, 'It is fulfilled.'

It was now about the sixth hour and the sun's light failed, so that darkness came over the whole land until the ninth hour. And Jesus cried out in a loud voice, 'Eloi, eloi, lama sabachthani?' which means, 'My God, my God, why have you forsaken me?' When some of those who stood by heard this, they said, 'Listen, he is calling on Elijah.' Someone ran and soaked a sponge in vinegar and, putting it on a reed, gave it to him to drink, saying 'Wait! And see if Elijah will come to take him down.' But Jesus cried out in a loud voice saying, 'Father, into your hands I commit my spirit.' With these words he bowed his head and breathed his last. And the veil of the Sanctuary was torn in two from top to bottom.

The centurion, who was standing in front of him, had seen how he had died, and he said, 'In truth this man was Son of God.'

From: *Mark* 15. *Luke* 23. *John* 19.

∽The Resurrection∾

After this, Joseph of Arimathea, who was a disciple of Jesus - though a secret one because he was afraid of the Jews - asked Pilate to let him remove the body of Jesus. Pilate gave permission, so they came and took it away. Nicodemus came as well - the same one who had first come to Jesus at night-time - and he brought a mixture of myrrh and aloes, weighing about a hundred pounds. They took the body of Jesus and bound it in linen clothes with the spices, following the Jewish burial custom. At the place where he had been crucified there was a garden, and in this garden a new tomb in which no one had yet been buried. Since it was the Jewish Day of Preparation and the tomb was nearby, they laid Jesus there.

Next day, that is when the Preparation Day was over, the chief priests and the Pharisees went in a body to Pilate and said to him, 'Your Excellency, we recall that this imposter said, while he was still alive, "After three days I shall rise again." Therefore give the order to have the sepulchre kept secure until the third day, for fear his disciples come and steal him away and tell the people, "He has risen from the dead." This last piece of fraud would be worse than what went before.' Pilate said to them, 'You may have your guard; go and make all secure as you know how.' So they went and made the sepulchre secure, putting seals on the stone and mounting a guard.

When the Sabbath was over, Mary of Magdala, Mary the mother of James, and Salome, bought spices with which to go and anoint him. And very early in the morning on the first day of the week they went to the tomb when the sun had risen. They had been saying to one another, 'Who will roll away the stone for us from the entrance to the tomb?'

And suddenly there was a violent earthquake, for an angel of the Lord, descending from heaven, came and rolled away the stone and sat on it. His face was like lightning, his robe white as snow. The guards were so shaken by fear of him that they were like dead men. But the angel spoke: and he said to the women, 'There is no need for you to be afraid. I know you are looking for Jesus, who was crucified. He is not here, for he has risen as he said he would. Come and see the place where he lay, then go quickly and tell his disciples, "He has risen from the dead and now he is going ahead of you to Galilee; that is where you will see him." Look! I have told you.' Filled with awe and great joy the women came quickly away from the tomb and ran to tell his disciples.

So Peter set out with the other disciple to go to the tomb. They ran together, but the other disciple, running faster than Peter, reached the tomb first; he bent down and saw the linen cloths lying on the

ground, but did not go in. Simon Peter, following him,
also came up, went into the tomb, saw the linen
cloths lying on the ground and also the cloth that had
been over his head; this was not with the linen cloths
but rolled up in a place by itself. Then the other
disciple who had reached the tomb first also went in;
he saw and he believed. Till this moment they had not
understood the scripture, that he must rise from the
dead. The disciples then went back home.

But Mary was standing outside the tomb, weeping.
Then, as she wept, she stooped to look inside, and
saw two angels in white sitting where the body of
Jesus had been, one at the head, the other at the feet.
They said, 'Woman, why are you weeping?' 'They
have taken my Lord away,' she replied, 'and I don't
know where they have put him.' As she said this she
turned round and saw Jesus standing there, though
she did not realise that it was Jesus. Jesus said to her,
'Woman why are you weeping? Who are you looking
for?' Supposing him to be the gardener, she said, 'Sir,
if you have taken him away, tell me where you have
put him, and I will go and remove him.' Jesus said,
'Mary!' She turned round then and said to him in
Hebrew, 'Rabbuni!' - which means Master. Jesus said
to her, 'Do not cling to me, because I have not yet
ascended to the Father. But go and find my brothers,
and tell them: I am ascending to my Father and your

Father, to my God and your God.' So Mary of Magdala told the disciples, 'I have seen the Lord,' and that he had said these things to her.

From: *John*: 19, 38 - 42. *Matthew*: 27, 62 -66. *Mark*: 16, 1-3

Matthew: 28, 2 - 8. *John*: 20, 3 - 18

∽

42

⟡Easter⟡

On Easter day, the church tells us that Jesus Christ made that journey to the ends of the universe for our sake. In the impenetrable gloom of death Christ came like light – the night became as bright as day and the darkness became as light. And so the Church can rightly consider these words of thanksgiving and trust as words spoken by the Risen Lord to his father: "Yes, I have journeyed to the uttermost depths of the earth, to the abyss of death, and have brought them light; now I have risen and I am upheld for ever by your hands."

But these words of the Risen Christ to the Father have also become words which the Lord speaks to each of us: "I arose and now I am still with you. My hand upholds you. I am present even at the door of death and there for you I will change darkness into light."

From: *Benedict XVI, Easter Vigil Homily*, April 2007.

∞

In his farewell discourse, Jesus announced his imminent death and resurrection to his disciples with these mysterious words: "I go away, and I will come to you." Dying is a "going away." In the case of our own death, the "going away" is definitive, there is no return.

For Jesus, on the other hand, his going ushers in a completely new and greater way of being present. By dying he enters into the love of the Father. His dying is an act of love. Love however is immortal. Therefore, his going away is transformed into a new coming, into a form of presence which reaches deeper and does not come to an end.

From: *Benedict XVI, Easter Vigil Homily*, March 2008.

∞

An ancient Jewish legend from the apocryphal book "The life of Adam and Eve" lays bare the whole of humanity's anguish at the destiny of illness, pain and death that has been imposed upon us. Man's resistance to death becomes evident: somewhere – people have constantly thought – there must be some cure for death. Sooner or later it should be possible to find the remedy not only for this or that illness, but for our ultimate destiny – for death itself. Surely the medicine of immortality must exist.

Indeed, the cure for death does exist. Christ is the tree of life, once more within our reach. If we remain close to him, then we have life. Hence during this night of resurrection, with all our hearts we shall sing the alleluia, the song of joy that has no need of words. Joy cannot be commanded. It can only be given. The risen Lord gives us joy: true life. We are already held for ever in the love of the One to whom all power in heaven and on earth has been given.

From: *Benedict XVI, Easter Vigil Homily*, April 2010.

∽

Certainly Job could complain before God about the presence of incomprehensible and apparently unjustified suffering in the world. In his pain he cried out: "Oh, that I knew where I might find him!" Often we cannot understand why God refrains from intervening. Yet he does not prevent us from crying out, like Jesus on the Cross: "My God, my God, why have you forsaken me?" We should continue asking this question in prayerful dialogue before his face.

Our protest is not meant to challenge God, or to suggest that error, weakness or indifference can be found in him. Instead, our crying out is, as it was for Jesus on the Cross, the deepest and most radical way of affirming our faith in his sovereign power. Even in their bewilderment and failure to understand the world around them, immersed like everyone else in the dramatic complexity of historical events, Christians remain unshakably certain that God is our Father and loves us, even when his silence remains incomprehensible.

From: *Benedict XVI, Encyclical Deus Caritas Est,*
God is Love, 2006

∽

⌒

The belief that love can reach into the afterlife, that reciprocal giving and receiving is possible, in which our affection for one another continues beyond the limits of death – this has been a fundamental conviction of Christianity throughout the ages and it remains a source of comfort today. Who would not feel the need to convey to their departed loved ones a sign of kindness, a gesture of gratitude or even a request for pardon?

Our lives are involved with one another, through innumerable interactions they are linked together. It is never too late to touch the heart of another, nor is it ever in vain. Our hope is always essentially also hope for others; only thus is it hope for me too. As Christians we should never limit ourselves to asking: how can I save myself? We should also ask: what can I do in order that others may be saved and that for them too the star of hope may rise? Then I will have done my utmost for my own personal salvation as well.

From: *Benedict XVI, Encyclical Spe Salvi,*
On Christian Hope, 2007

⌒

⌦From the Dream of Gerontius⌦

Gerontius

Jesu, Maria! I am near to death,
  And Thou art calling me; I know it now.
 Not by the token of this faltering breath,
This chill at heart, this dampness on my brow, -
(Jesu, have mercy! Mary, pray for me!)
"Tis this new feeling, never felt before,
(Be with me, Lord, in my extremity!)
That I am going, that I am no more.
'Tis this strange innermost abandonment,
(Lover of Souls! great God! I look to Thee,)
This emptying out of each constituent
And natural force, by which I come to be.
Pray for me, O my friends, a visitant
Is knocking his dire summons at my door,
The like of whom, to scare me and to daunt,
Has never, never come to me before;
'Tis death - O loving friends,
your prayers! - 'tis he! ...
As though my very being had given way,
As though I was no more a substance now,
And could fall back on nought to be my stay,
(Help, loving Lord! Thou my sole Refuge, Thou,)
And turn no wither, but must needs decay

And drop from out this universal frame
Into that shapeless, scopeless, blank abyss,
That utter nothingness, of which I came,
That is it that has come to pass in me;
Oh horror! this it is, my dearest, this;
So pray for me, my friends,
who have not strength to pray.

∞

Assistants

Be merciful, be gracious: spare him, Lord.
Be merciful, be gracious: Lord deliver him.
From the sins that are past;
From Thy frown and Thine ire;
From the perils of dying:
From any complying with sin, or denying
His God, or relying On self, at the last;
From the nethermost fire; From all that is evil;
From power of the devil;
Thy servant deliver, For once and for ever.
By Thy birth, and by Thy Cross,
Rescue him from endless loss;
By Thy death and burial, Save him from a final fall;
By Thy rising from the tomb, By Thy mounting up
above, By the Spirit's gracious love,
Save him in the day of doom.

∞

The Priest

Go forth upon thy journey, Christian soul!
Go from this world! Go, in the Name of God,
The Omipotent Father, who created thee!
Go, in the name of Jesus Christ, our Lord,
Son of the living God, who bled for thee!
Go, in the name of the Holy Spirit, who
Hath been poured out on thee! Go, in the name
of Angels and Archangels: in the name
of Thrones and Dominations; in the name
of Princedoms and of Powers; and in the name
of Cherubim and Seraphim, go forth!
Go, in the name of Patriarchs and Prophets;
and of Apostles and Evangelists;
of Martyrs and Confessors; in the name
of Holy Monks and Hermits; in the name
of Holy Virgins; and all Saints of God,
Both men and women, go! Go on thy course!
And may thy place to-day be found in peace,
And may thy dwelling be the Holy Mount
of Sion - through the Name of Christ, our Lord.

∞

Soul

Take me away, and in the lowest deep
There let me be, and there in hope the lone night
watches keep, Told out for me.
There, motionless and happy in my pain,
Lone, not forlorn, - There will I sing my sad perpetual
strain, Until the morn.
There will I sing, and soothe my stricken breast,
Which ne'er can cease to throb, and pine, and
languish, till possest of its Sole Peace.
There will I sing my absent Lord and Love: -
Take me away,
That sooner I may rise, and go above,
And see Him in the truth of everlasting day.

∞

Souls in Purgatory

Lord, Thou hast been our refuge:
in every generation;
Before the hills were born, and the world
was: from age to age Thou art God.
Bring us not, Lord, very low: for Thou
has said, Come back again, ye sons of Adam.
A thousand years before Thine eyes are
as but yesterday: and as a watch of

the night which is come and gone.
Though the grass spring up in the morning:
yet in the evening it shall shrivel up and die.
Thus we fail in Thine anger: and in Thy
wrath are we troubled.
Thou has set our sins in Thy sight:
and our round of days in the light
of Thy countenance. Come back, O Lord!
how long: and be entreated for Thy servants.
in Thy morning we shall be filled with
Thy mercy: we shall rejoice and be
in pleasure all our days.
We shall be glad according to the days
of our humiliation: and the years in
which we have seen evil.Look, O Lord, upon Thy
servants and
on Thy work: and direct their children.
And let the beauty of the Lord our
God be upon us: and the work of our
hands, establish Thou it.
Glory be to the Father, and to the Son
and to the Holy Ghost.
As it was in the beginning, is now,
and ever shall be: world without end.
Amen.

Angel

Softly and gently, dearly-ransomed soul,
In my most loving arms I now enfold thee,
And o'er the penal waters, as they roll,
I poise thee, and I lower thee, and hold thee.

And carefully I dip thee in the lake,
And thou, without a sob or a resistance,
Dost through the flood thy rapid passage take,
Sinking deep, deeper, into the dim distance.

Angels, to whom the willing task is given,
Will tend, and nurse, and lull thee as thou liest;
And Masses on the earth, and prayers in heaven,
Shall aid thee at the Throne of the Most Highest.

Farewell, but not for ever! brother dear,
Be brave and patient on thy bed of sorrow;
Swiftly shall pass thy night of trial here,
And I will come and wake thee on the morrow.

John Henry Newman 1801 – 90.

∽Hymns∽

*A*bide with me; fast falls the eventide;
The darkness deepens; Lord, with me abide!
When other helpers fail, and comforts flee,
Help of the helpless, O abide with me.

Swift to its close ebbs out life's little day;
Earths joys grow dim, its glories pass away;
Change and decay in all around I see;
O thou who changest not, abide with me.

I need they presence every passing hour;
What but they grace can foil the tempters power?
Who like thyself my guide and stay can be?
Through cloud and sunshine, O abide with me.

I have no foe with thee at hand to bless;
Ills have no weight, and tears no bitterness.
Where is death's sting? where, grave, thy victory?
I triumph still, if thou abide with me.

Hold thou thy Cross before my closing eyes
Shine through the gloom, and point me to the skies;
Heaven's morning breaks, and earth's vain shadows
flee; In life, in death, O Lord, abide with me!

H. F. Lyte, 1793 - 1847.

∽

∞

The Pillar of the cloud

Lead, Kindly Light, amid the encircling gloom,
Lead Thou me on!
The night is dark,
and I am far from home
Lead Thou me on!
Keep Thou my feet, I do not ask to see
The distant scene, one step enough for me.

I was not ever thus, nor pray'd that Thou
Shouldst lead me on.
I loved to choose and see my path, but now
Lead Thou me on!
I loved the garish day, and, spite of fears,
Pride ruled my will: remember not past years.

So long Thy power hath blest me, sure it stil
Will lead me on,
O'er moor and fen, o'er crag and torrent, till
The night is gone;
And with the morn those Angel faces smile
Which I have loved long since, and lost awhile.

J. H. Newman, 1801 – 90.

∞

∽

*M*y God, I love thee: not because
I hope for heaven thereby,
Nor yet because who love thee not
Are lost eternally.

Thou, O my Jesus, thou didst me
Upon the Cross embrace;
For me didst bear the nails and spear,
And manifold disgrace,

And griefs and torments numberless,
and sweat of agony;
E'en death itself; and all for one
Who was thine enemy.

Then why, O blessed Jesu Christ,
Should I not love thee well,
Not for the sake of winning heaven,
Or of escaping hell;

Not with the hope of gaining aught,
Not seeking a reward;
But as thyself has loved me,
O ever-loving Lord!

E'en so I love thee, and will love,
And in thy praise will sing,
Solely because thou art my God,
And my eternal king.

    Saint Francis Xavier. 1506 - 52. Translated *E. Caswall.*

∽

∞

Glory be to the Father,
and to the Son,
and to the Holy Spirit,
As it was in the beginning,
is now, and ever shall be,
world without end.
Amen

∞

May the peace of the Lord
be always with you.

∞

Biblical texts are based on The New Jerusalem Bible, Darton Longman and Todd, 1985. Translations of the Psalms are based on The Grail Psalter, The Grail/Harper Collins 1962. Hymns from The English Hymnal, 1906. Extracts of the Dream of Gerontius, Oxford Edition of the poems of John Henry Newman, 1914.